THE FISH
who could wish

For Carl and Kerri-Leigh
JB

For the Tzannes family
KP

This edition is published by special arrangement with Kane/Miller
Book Publishers.

Grateful acknowledgment is made to Kane/Miller Book Publishers for
permission to reprint *The Fish Who Could Wish* by John Bush, illustrated by
Korky Paul. Text copyright © 1991 by John Bush; illustrations copyright
© 1991 by Korky Paul.

Printed in Mexico

ISBN 0-15-302138-1

2 3 4 5 6 7 8 9 10   050   97 96 95 94 93

THE FISH
who could wish

JOHN BUSH & KORKY PAUL

HARCOURT BRACE & COMPANY
Orlando Atlanta Austin Boston San Francisco Chicago Dallas New York
Toronto London

In the deep blue sea,
In the deep of the blue,
Swam a fish who could wish,
And each wish would come true.
Oh the fun that he had!
Oh the things he would do!
Just wishing away
In the deep water blue.

He wished for a castle.

He wished for a car.

He wished for a horse
And a Spanish guitar.

Once, when he wished
He could go out and ski
It snowed for a week
Under the sea.

He wished he could fly
And to his delight,
Flew twice round the world
In exactly one night!

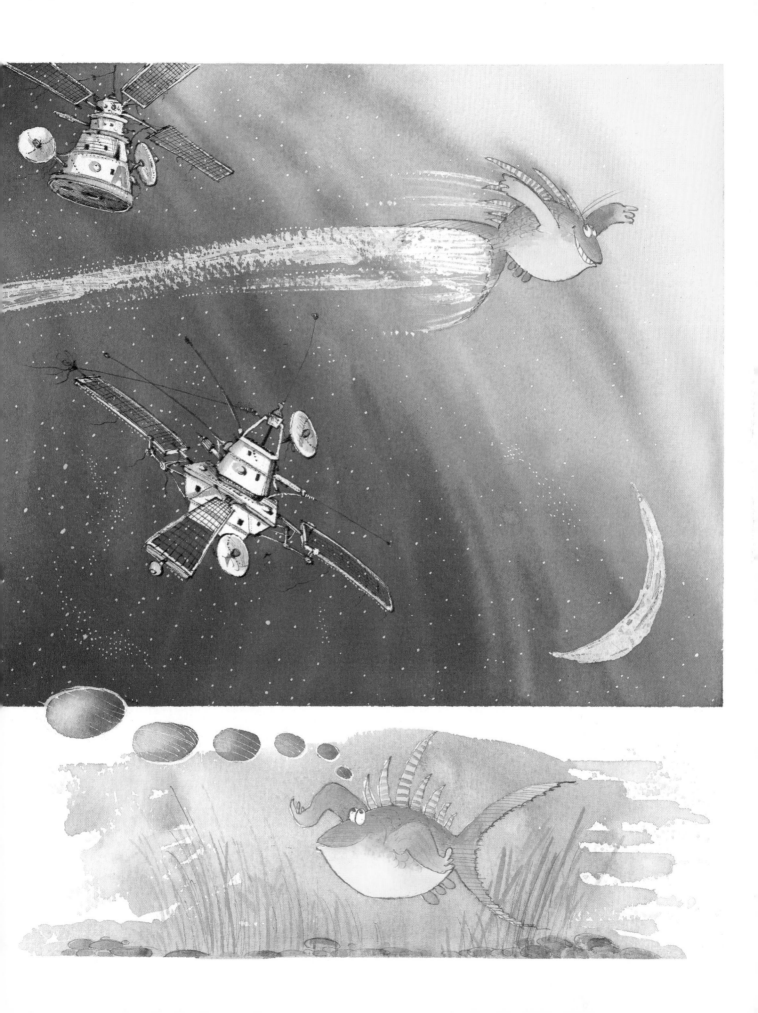

If sharks came a-hunting
For a nice fishy treat,
He'd quickly just wish
He was too small to eat.

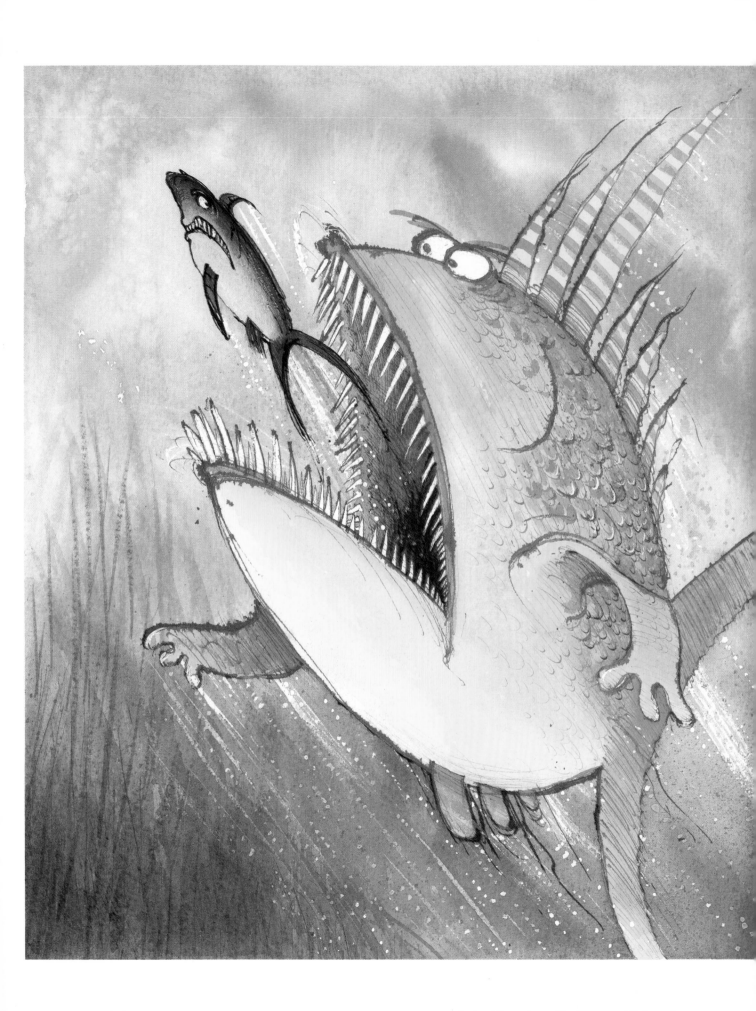

And to teach sharks a lesson,
Do you know what he'd wish?
That he was a shark
And the shark was a fish!

He'd wish himself square,
Or round as a biscuit,
Triangular, oval . . .
Name it, he wished it.

He wished for fine suits
And handsome silk ties,
But the one thing he never wished
Was to be wise . . .

One day, just for fun,
That silly old fish
Wished the silliest, silliest
Wish he could wish.

That silly old fish
Wished he could be
Just like all the other
Fish in the sea.
But wishing was something
Other fish could not do.
So that was his very last
wish that came true.